The Brain of a Legend

Amanda Myers

Cover and interior illustrations: Chad Thompson

Printed in the United States of America

Published by Braughler Books LLC., Springboro, Ohio

First printing, 2024

ISBN: 978-1-955791-99-1

Library of Congress Control Number: Pending

Ordering information: Special discounts are available on quantity purchases by bookstores,corporations, associations, and others.

For details, contact the publisher at:
sales@braughlerbooks.com or at 937-58-BOOKS

Braughler™ Books
braughlerbooks.com

This book is dedicated to my own legend, Charlie, and his heaven-sent protector, my daughter Allison

All are made special and unique
like unicorns and superheroes.

The part that makes you unique is your gift.

Some are fast. Some can build. Some can even work together on a team.

What is your gift?_____

But let's not forget
about my Legend . . .

My legend,
along with many
others have a gift of
a special brain called Autism.

With Autism,
you see the world differently.

Lights may be too bright;
sounds may be too loud, or
clothes may feel too itchy.

Some may flap their hands.
Some may repeat themselves . . . over and over.
While others may be very picky eaters.

But all with Autism are
unique and special just like you!

Those with Autism
have gifts too. It just
may take extra time for
them to show you.

My legend is a _____

Together our gifts make a more beautiful world.

Can you use your gift to help someone with a special brain of Autism? _____

Some days those with a special brain may not answer.

Some days those with a special brain may not want to play.

But those with a special brain are always listening to you and know you care.

How can you help someone with a special brain of Autism?_____

Help each other
be the best unicorns and
superheroes you can be to all our friends . . .

Like my legend_____

About the Author

My name is Amanda Myers, and I am a wife and mother to two children. The doctors diagnosed our son with autism around age two. Finding a constructive way for the young children in our son's life to ask about autism, without making it solely about our differences, has been a struggle for me. This journey led me to writing this book in hopes it helps families give children an outlet to ask questions and feed their curiosity. I feel the more we answer and contribute to their knowledge about autism, the more inclusion and friendships that will transpire.

While it's challenging, being a parent to a child with autism has been the most rewarding rollercoaster ride of my life. I aim to keep riding and promoting acceptance and inclusion for my son and others.

www.ingramcontent.com/pod-product-compliance
Lightning Source LLC
Chambersburg PA
CBHW060858090426
42737CB00023B/3489